MORMON DOCTRINES
IN LIGHT OF THE BIBLE

By
Rick DeMichele, Pastor
Treasure Valley Baptist Church
Meridian, ID 83642
Copyright © 2015

Published by TVBC
1300 S. Teare Ave.
Meridian, ID 83642
(208) 888-4545
Please visit our web site at www.tvbc.org

DayStar Publishing
1-800-311-1823
www.daystarpublishing.com

2015 Editing and Cover Design
Truth and Song Christian Bookstore
www.truthandsong.com

ISBN: 9781942050001
Library of Congress: 2015947176

TABLE OF CONTENTS

CHAPTER ONE
FINAL AUTHORITY

By what authority doest thou these things? Since there are so many creeds and religions in this world, the question posed in Mark 11 is an important one. As Bible believing Christians, we believe in ONE FINAL AUTHORITY - THE BIBLE. All doctrine, whether it be Mormon, Catholic, Buddhist, or Baptist is judged in one court of appeals - God's word. If a doctrine lines up with scripture, it is of God; if not, it is of man or Satan. There are no other possibilities (Isaiah 8:20).

All man-made religions have multiple final authorities, and expediency will determine which is used in a given situation. For example, in a Catholic publication put out by the Knights of Columbus, under the teaching about the *Mother Mary* we read:

67 a. At the same time, the Council exhorts scholars and preachers to take a sane course between exaggeration and narrowmindedness. As guides, let them take the Sacred Scriptures, the holy fathers and doctors, the various liturgies and the teaching authority of the Church.

The above is taken from a layman's account of Vatican II. In it the Catholic is exhorted to use five different sources to determine doctrine.

The Mormon church also has five final authorities, they are: the Book of Mormon, Pearl of Great Price, Doctrine and Covenants, the Bible, and the word of living Apostles and prophets. In this study, we will examine the Mormon teachings on the authority of the Book of Mormon, Pearl of Great Price, Doctrine and Covenants, and the Bible. The subjects of living Apostles and prophecies will be taken up in a later chapter.

I. THE BIBLE

Let's examine several scriptures to see what the Bible says about itself:

A. Psalms 119:89 - God's word, eternal

B. Psalms 12:6, 7 - Pure and preserved forever

C. II Timothy 3:16 - Inspired and profitable

D. II Peter 1:21 - Given by the Holy Ghost

through holy men of God.

The Bible believing Christian accepts the 66 books of the Old and New Testaments as God's final authority for faith and practice. Does the well-taught Mormon do the same? Let's see what Mormonism teaches about the Bible. One of the accusations often made by the Mormon critic of the Bible is that it has had many plain and precious parts removed. In fact, Joseph Smith said that he believed the Bible as it read when it came *from the pen of the original writers*. He also claimed that ignorant translators, careless transcribers, or designing and corrupt priests *have committed many errors*.

Even the Book of Mormon claims that the Bible has been tampered with and changed:

...for behold, they have taken away from the gospel of the Lamb many parts which are plain and precious; and also many covenants of the Lord have they taken away. And all this have they done that they might pervert the right ways of the Lord, and they might blind the eyes and harden the hearts of the children of men. I Nephi 13:26b-27

The Articles of Faith, number eight states:

We believe the Bible to be the word of God as far as it is translated correctly; we also believe the Book of Mormon to be the word of God.

The following passage taken from the Book of Mormon (II Nephi 29:6) is especially revealing of the official Mormon attitude toward the scriptures:

Thou fool, that shall say: A Bible, we have got a Bible, and we need no more Bible. (See also verse ten of the same chapter.)

It should be obvious by now that the Mormon church does not hold the Bible to be THE FINAL WORD OF GOD the way a born-again, Bible believing Christian does.

II. THE BOOK OF MORMON

The Book of Mormon claims to be a book much like the Bible. It covers a period of time from 600 B.C. to A.D. 421. It is a series of books telling of the life and descendants of Lehi, a man of Jerusalem. It is a series of claimed revelations and historical accounts given by men during this thousand year period of time.

Joseph Smith said that he was told about the book by God, who directed him to find it and translate it from the golden plates upon which it had been written. The work of translation was accomplished by Joseph Smith, wearing divine glasses, and looking through these glasses into a hat. As he translated the material, and had it recorded by his scribe to God's satisfaction, the image in the glasses would fade away and a new image would come in its place.

The *three witnesses* bear testimony to the accuracy of the fact of the gold plates, and that they were translated into English by Joseph Smith:

Be it known unto all nations, kindreds, tongues, and people, unto whom this work shall come: That we, through the grace of God the Father, and our Lord Jesus Christ, have seen the plates which contains this record, which is a record of the people of Nephi, and also of the Lamanites, their brethren, and also of the people of Jared, who came from the tower of which hath been spoken. And we also know that they have been translated by the gift and power of God, for his voice hath declared it unto us; wherefore we know of a surety that the work is true. Book of Mormon, The Testimony of Three

Witnesses, p. vii.

The Bible claims to be inspired, as written by its original writers. Since that time it has been copied, and recopied, and translated numerous times. The remarkable thing about the Bible is that though it has come from ancient times, its accuracy has been perfectly preserved. But, when checking two editions of the Book of Mormon, it is shocking to find that it contains nearly four thousand changes. For the most part they were not serious theological errors, but errors of grammar, chronology, and in general, evidences of ignorance. Some have blamed these errors on the printer. Certainly one must have been hard up to find a printer if he would have had to be willing to accept a book that had an average of 7.6 errors on each side of each page. It is also interesting that with a prophet around, it still took until 1921 to get most of the errors out of the text. The errors are consistent in form, thoroughly integrated throughout the whole, and definitely not of a type we could blame on the printer. Since it was supposedly translated by the prophet, with God's help, we would expect it to be as Joseph Smith said it was: *the most correct book on the earth.*

Some serious errors still exist. For example, THE

BOOK OF MORMON SAYS THAT JESUS WAS
BORN IN JERUSALEM (Alma 7:10).

Other works have been done that deal completely
with the textual problems of the Book of Mormon.
It is interesting that such a work would have 3,913
changes from the first until the present edition. If
such textual problems were found in the Bible, it
would leave serious doubts as to its inspiration.

The Book of Mormon presents many textual
problems. First, and probably foremost, is the
extensive quotations from the King James Bible.
Since the Book of Mormon covers a period of time
from 600 B.C. to A.D. 421, how could it quote from
a book that was not translated until A.D. 1611?
The problem is readily apparent; either the King
James translators copied from the Book of
Mormon, or the writers of the Book of Mormon
copied from the translators of the King James
Bible. How could one believe the Book of
Mormon was really finished in A.D. 421 when it so
often quotes from a book translated so many years
later? Of course, one could answer that God gave
the same revelation to the people in America that
He did in Palestine. Would He give it in the exact
King James English both times? Would He use the
exact words of Isaiah, Peter, and Paul? In fact,

would He make the Book of Mormon about one third a direct quotation from the King James Bible? It is interesting that the English of the Book of Mormon becomes markedly improved when it is time to quote from the Bible.

What can we say about these things? To persons familiar with the study of literature, particularly ancient literature, they immediately become suspicious that the author of the Book of Mormon had in his hands a copy of the King James Bible. In fact, after making a careful study of the two books, it seems impossible to draw any other conclusion. Many beautiful passages from the Bible are copied over into the Book of Mormon. For example, check the references about *faith, hope, and charity*. Paul's beautiful writing in I Corinthians 13 is borrowed and reborrowed. A careful reading will reveal that the Book of Mormon borrows most of the Bible stories, supplying different names, and fits them into another time and place. Literally hundreds of examples could be supplied.

This is the *further revelation of God* that Mormon missionaries try to get the unsuspecting prospect to read. While many have sought for a *burning in the bosom*, they should be looking for honest, historical, and accurate credibility in a book that is supposed to be on a par with the word of God!

III. THE DOCTRINE AND COVENANTS

The Doctrine and Covenants is a series of revelations, supposedly given to Joseph Smith, with minor additions by later successors in the presidency of the Latter-day Saints.

The first revelation, according to his own testimony, was given to Joseph Smith in September of 1823, and he received the last in June of 1844. There is one section given by Brigham Young, and short notes by Presidents Wilford Woodruff and Lorenzo Snow.

For the most part, the Doctrine and Covenants is the work of Joseph Smith. The Doctrine and Covenants introduces many of the different doctrinal ideas that are taught by the Mormon Church. It is the Doctrine and Covenants that makes the Mormon Church so different from most other religious bodies in America. Serious theological problems come from this book. The Doctrine and Covenants is even more difficult for Latter-day Saints to defend than the Book of Mormon.

While the Book of Mormon is a book about the size of our Old Testament, the Doctrine and Covenants is about the size of the New Testament.

The very first section of the Doctrine and Covenants tells us that these revelations are from God:

What I the Lord have spoken, I have spoken, and I excuse not myself; and though the heavens and the earth pass away, my word shall not pass away, but shall all be fulfilled, whether by my own voice or by the voice of my servants, it is the same. For behold, and lo, the Lord is God, and the Spirit beareth record, and the record is true, and the truth abideth forever and ever. Amen. Doctrine and Covenants 1:38-39

The Doctrine and Covenants teaches the following anti-Biblical doctrines:

A. Vegetarianism – D. & C. 89:12-15

B. Polytheism - D. & C. 121:28; 132:19,20

C. Polygamy - D. & C. 132:1,3,4,38-40,61,62

D. The true church ceased to exist until it was restored by Joseph Smith - D. & C. 20:1,2

E. God the Father has a physical body - D. & C. 130:22

F. Genealogical research for the dead – D. & C. 128:24

These are only a sampling of the doctrines taught in the Doctrine and Covenants that are an outright affront to the word of God. How can two works that are in disagreement both be thought to be God's word?

IV. <u>THE PEARL OF GREAT PRICE</u>

The Pearl of Great Price is a small volume made up of three parts; the books of Moses, Abraham, and Joseph Smith. It is this volume that presents the most damaging evidence against Joseph Smith. In this volume we have proof positive that Joseph Smith was not capable of translating any foreign document.

The book of Abraham begins with a few comments in the heading above the text which says:

A translation of some ancient records, that have fallen into our hands from the catacombs of Egypt - The writings of Abraham while he was in Egypt, called the Book of Abraham, <u>written by his own hand, upon papyrus</u>.

This would be fantastic information if it were true. Can you imagine having the very own handwriting of *father Abraham*? It would be the only instance of an original handwritten document of any Bible writer. We are immediately skeptical since Abraham lived so long ago, and we do not have any other Bible author's original manuscript.

We will not waste the time to argue against such a foolish claim. There is no doubt that someone has followed *cunningly devised fables* (II Peter. 1:16).

Our Lord Jesus Christ defines the cannon of the true word of God, the one and only final authority of God, in Luke 24:44. Note the solemn warning given to those who would add to the content of holy writ (Revelation 22:18, 19).

For further reading, see Gerald and Sandra Tanner's definitive works, <u>Mormonism, Shadow or Reality?</u> and <u>3,913 changes in the Book of Mormon.</u>

Chapter Two
THE NATURE OF GOD

Every religion has a foundation; part of this foundation includes a concept of the nature of God. Without a proper biblical concept of the nature of God, the salvation offered by any religion will be of no profit (Hebrews 11:6). Faith itself is not as important as THE OBJECT OF FAITH. As we examine what Mormonism and the Bible teach about the nature of God, let's keep in mind that no matter how sincere one may be, and no matter how much faith one exercises in a false god, a false god cannot save from sin and hell!

I.   THE MORMON CHALLENGE

Historically, Mormons themselves have challenged us to examine their doctrines in light of the Bible and prove their verity or falsehood. Joseph Fielding Smith, tenth president of the Mormon Church said:

If Joseph Smith was a deceiver, who willfully attempted to mislead the people, then he should be exposed; his claims should be refuted, and his doctrines shown to be false, for THE DOCTRINES

OF AN IMPOSTER CANNOT BE MADE TO HARMONIZE IN ALL PARTICULARS WITH DIVINE TRUTH. If his claims and declarations were built upon fraud and deceit, there would appear many errors and contradictions which would be easy to detect. The doctrines of false teachers will not stand the test when tried by the accepted standards of measurement, the scriptures. Doctrines of Salvation by Joseph Fielding Smith, Vol. 1, pg. 188

Brigham Young also set forth the challenges:

Take up the Bible, compare the religion of the Latter-Day Saints with it and see if it will stand the test. Journal of Discourses, Vol. 16, Pg. 46, May 18, 1873

No man can disprove a truth...why not rather every man rise up and say, 'Let God be true, let the truth remain, and let me know the truth; that is what I want, - I will submit to it; and let every false theory and principle fall, to rise no more?' Journal of Discourses, Vol. 8, Pg. 132, July 22, 1860

Even more to the point was Orson Pratt's statement regarding truth:

If we cannot convince you by reason, nor by the word of God, that your religion is wrong we will not persecute you...we ask from you the same generosity...Convince us of our errors of doctrine, if we have any, by reason, by logical arguments, or by the word of God, and we will be ever grateful for the information, and you will ever have the pleasing reflection that you have been instruments in the hands of God of redeeming your fellow beings from the darkness which you may see enveloping their minds. The Seer, pg. 15, 16

II. THE BIBLICAL DESCRIPTION OF GOD

What is God like? Where did He come from? Does He have flesh and bones, or is He a spirit? If you are saved and familiar with the teachings of the Bible concerning the nature of God, you probably take for granted the answers to the aforementioned questions.

Many who assume that Mormonism is just another Christian denomination don't realize just how unorthodox the Mormon doctrines about God really are.

The Bible teaches us about a one and only, eternal, omnipotent, omnipresent, omniscient, immutable

God who is also, holy, just, and incorruptible. HE IS WITHOUT PEERS OF ANY KIND AT ALL.

Consider the following verses:

I am He: before me there was no God formed, neither shall there be after me. I, even I, am the Lord; and beside me there is no Saviour. Isaiah 43:10, 11

I am the first, and I am the last; and beside Me there is no God. Isaiah 44:6

God is a Spirit: and they that worship him must worship him in spirit and in truth. John 4:24

For when God made promise to Abraham, because he could swear by no greater, he sware by himself. Hebrews 6:13

For I am the Lord, I change not. Malachi 3:6

No man hath seen God at any time; the only begotten Son, which is in the bosom of the Father, he hath declared him. John 1:18

See also the following texts to show the exclusiveness of our God: Exodus 3:14; Numbers

23:19; Isaiah 44:7, 8; 45:5, 6, 21; 46:9; and I Timothy 1:17.

III. <u>THE MORMON DESCRIPTION OF GOD</u>

Does a faithful Mormon, who believes what his church teaches about God, accept the above mentioned verses as the final word about God, His character, and nature? The answer is no. To those who have only encountered the clean-cut Mormon missionaries, who insist that they too believe the Bible, the following excerpts taken from Mormon sources may come as a surprise:

The Father has a body of flesh and bones as tangible as man's; the Son also. Doctrines and Covenants 130:22

Joseph Smith also declared:

God Himself was once as we are now, and is an exalted MAN, and sits enthroned in yonder heavens!....I am going to tell you how God came to be God. We have imagined and supposed that God was God from all eternity. I will refute that idea, and take away the veil, so that you may see. Teachings of the Prophet Joseph Smith, by Joseph Fielding Smith, Pg. 345

Mormon teaching on the nature of God can be capsulated by their oft repeated saying:

As man is, God once was; as God is, man may become.

These statements are nothing less than blasphemy! See Romans 1:22, 23 for God's own indictment on such teachings.

Lest we be accused of slander, consider these oft quoted statements attributed to Joseph Smith:

God himself was once as we are now, and is an exalted man...if you were to see him today, you would see him like a man in form - like yourselves, in all the person, image, and very form as a man,...you have got to learn how to be Gods yourselves...the same as all Gods have done before you. Teachings of the Prophet Joseph Smith, by Joseph Fielding Smith, Pg. 345, 346

We believe in a God who is Himself progressive, whose majesty is intelligence; whose perfection consists in eternal advancement - a Being who has attained His exalted state by a path which now His children are permitted to follow, whose glory it is their heritage to share. In spite of the opposition of the sects, in the face of direct charges of blasphemy, the Church proclaims the eternal truth: 'As man is, God once was; as God is, man may be.' The Articles of Faith, pg. 430

Mormon sources also teach the doctrine of POLYTHEISM:

Three separate personages - Father, Son, and Holy Ghost - comprise the Godhead. As each of these persons is a God, it is evident, from this standpoint alone, that a plurality of Gods exists. To us, speaking in the proper finite sense, these three are the only Gods we worship. But in addition there is an infinite number of holy personages, drawn from worlds without number, who have passed on to exaltation and are thus gods. Mormon Doctrine, by Bruce R. McConkie, pg. 576, 577

See also Doctrine and Covenants 121:28, 32.

What is very peculiar about this is that the Book of Mormon is largely a monotheistic book. See the following in the Book of Mormon, II Nephi 31:21; Moroni 8:18. In spite of this, we still recommend THE BIBLE AS THE ONLY SOURCE OF LIFE FOR LOST MORMONS, and THE MOST

IMPORTANT TOOL IN REACHING MORMONS FOR JESUS CHRIST.

In conclusion, we may safely say that in the Mormon mind, the image of God is that of a corruptible man who *progressed into Godhood*.

Mormon theology portrays God as a mortal man who lived, who died, was resurrected, and was given authority to become a God by some power greater than himself.   As we have seen, this concept of God is TOTALLY FOREIGN to the BIBLE.

Chapter Three
THE LORD JESUS CHRIST

We cannot overstate the importance of a religion's treatment of the person and work of the Lord Jesus Christ. In I John 2:1 we find that Christ is our ADVOCATE with the Father. If Mormonism has a warped view of the Saviour, it is a religion without an advocate, a creed that leaves the hopeless Mormon to plead his own case before a holy and perfect God.

The following verses show the gravity of error in regard to the person and work of our blessed Saviour: I John 2:21-24; 4:1-3; II John 7-11.

In this study we will focus primarily on the PERSON of Jesus Christ as found in scripture, and compare our findings with the teachings of Mormonism (II Corinthians 11:4). We will focus on the WORK of Christ in a later chapter.

I. BIBLICAL DESCRIPTION OF JESUS CHRIST

The Bible teaches us that God is a triune God (I John 5:7). There is one God who manifests Himself in three equal persons; the Father, the

Son, and the Holy Spirit. They are all equally God, though they are also distinctly individual. This Bible doctrine of the trinity is IMPOSSIBLE TO UNDERSTAND. The deity of Christ is called a MYSTERY (I Timothy 3:16). We do not have to be able to understand the Godhead, we must accept by FAITH what the Bible says about the Godhead.

Cultists have cut their spiritual jugular vein trying to shrink God down to their own understanding. Please keep in mind what the scriptures say about God the Father (chapter 2), as we discover that Jesus is also deity:

A. Genesis 1:1 - This verse coupled with Genesis 1:26; John 1:1-3 and Colossians 1:12-19 shows Christ's deity through the act of creation.

B. Isaiah 9:6 - *The mighty God, the everlasting father.*

C. John 1:1 - *The Word was God.*

D. John 8:58 - *Before Abraham was, I am.*

E. John 10:30 - *I and my father are one.*

F. I Timothy 3:16 - *God was manifest in the flesh.*

G.   Hebrews 1:8 - *But unto the Son, he saith, thy throne, O God.*

These are only a sampling of the scriptures that attribute to the Lord Jesus Christ equal claim to deity as the Father.

II. <u>MORMON DESCRIPTION OF JESUS CHRIST</u>

A. SPIRIT BROTHER OF LUCIFER

The following is what Milton R. Hunter, of the first Council of Seventy, indicated that Jesus is:

At the great council in heaven, God stood in the midst of His spirit-children and appointed 'the noble and great ones' to future positions of leadership after they should become mortals. In that assembled throng there was 'one like unto God'. This glorious personage volunteered to be the Savior of the world, humbly declaring, 'Father, Thy will be done, and the glory be thine forever'.   Thereupon the Father accepted His offer and foreordained Him to this great mission.   This individual, while acting as the mediator, was none other than Jehovah of the Old Testament, and when He lived in mortality He was Jesus Christ of the New Testament.   Michael the archangel, commonly known to us as Adam, was appointed to be the first mortal man; and Eve, a spirit of comparable brilliance and faithfulness, was assigned to be his helpmate - the 'Mother of all mortals'. Abraham, Isaiah, Jeremiah, Joseph Smith, and others of the holy prophets were foreordained to positions of leadership in their respective dispensations, and Mary was chosen to be the mother of the Son of God. These brilliant children of divine parents were chosen at the council in heaven for important work in the plan of salvation because of their intellectual superiority and their righteousness. They were foreordained, but not predestined to their respective positions of leadership in mortality.

The appointment of Jesus to be Savior of the world was contested by one of the other sons of God. He was called Lucifer, son of the morning. Haughty, ambitious, and covetous of power and glory, this spirit-brother of Jesus desperately tried to become the Savior of mankind. At the great council he proposed a new plan of salvation, one which was not based on eternal truth. The Gospel Through the Ages, pg. 15

The contention in heaven was - Jesus said there would be certain souls that would not be saved; and the devil said he could save them all, and laid his plans before the grand council, who gave their vote in favor of Jesus Christ. Teachings of the Prophet Joseph Smith, by Joseph Fielding Smith, pg. 357

This teaching is prevalent in Mormonism. How can Jesus be a *SPIRIT-BROTHER* of Lucifer, when Colossians 1:16 tells us that Christ created all things, including Lucifer himself (Ezekiel 28:13-15)?

B.   A GOD WHO WAS ONCE A MAN, WHO PROGRESSED TO GODHOOD

From the time of their spirit birth, the Father's pre-existent offspring were endowed with agency and subjected to the provisions of the laws ordained for their government.   They had power to obey or disobey and to progress in one field or another. 'The first principles of man are self-existent with God,' the Prophet said. 'God himself, finding he was in the midst of spirits and glory, because he was more intelligent, saw proper to institute laws whereby the rest could have a privilege to advance like himself.'

The pre-existent life was thus a period - undoubtedly an infinitely long on - of probation, progression, and schooling.   The spirit hosts were taught and given experiences in various administrative capacities. Some so exercised their agency and so conformed to law as to become 'noble and great'; these were foreordained before their mortal births to perform great missions for the Lord in this life. (Abraham 3:22-28) Christ, the Firstborn, was the mightiest of all the spirit children of the Father. (Doctrine and Covenants 93:21-23). Mortal progression and testing is a continuation of what began in pre-existence. Mormon Doctrine, by Bruce R. McConkie, pg. 590

The above quote claims that Christ attained unto Godhood, which means that He wasn't always God in the past. This Mormon teaching is quickly dismissed by comparing the following two scriptures:

1. *In the beginning was the Word, and Word was with God, and the Word was God.* John 1:1

2. *Even from everlasting to everlasting, thou art God.* Psalm 90:2

Jesus is God, and God always has been God! Instead of the man (Jesus) climbing the ladder of achievement to *Godhood* (man becoming God), God became man! That is, Jesus Christ became the God-man in His incarnation at the first advent.

Let this mind be in you, which was also in Christ Jesus: Who, being in the form of God, thought it not robbery to be equal with God: But made himself of no reputation, and took upon him the form of a servant, and was made in the likeness of men. Philippians 2:5-7

See also Isaiah 43:10, 11.

C. JESUS IS SEPARATE FROM THE FATHER, EXCEPT FOR ONENESS OF PURPOSE

Three separate personages - Father, Son and Holy Ghost - comprise the Godhead. As each of these persons is a God, it is evident, from this standpoint alone, that a plurality of Gods exists. To us, speaking in the proper finite sense, these three are the only Gods we worship. But in addition there is an infinite number of holy personages, drawn from worlds without number, who have passed on to exaltation and are thus gods. Mormon Doctrine, by Bruce R. McConkie, pg. 576, 577

If the Father and Son are as distinct in essence as

the Mormon church would have us believe, one wonders why the Savior said what He did in John 14:10, 11?

D. JESUS WAS NOT CONCEIVED BY THE HOLY SPIRIT

THE FIRSTBORN. Our Father in heaven is the Father of Jesus Christ, both in the spirit and in the flesh. Our Savior is the Firstborn in the spirit, the Only Begotten in the flesh.

CHRIST NOT BEGOTTEN OF THE HOLY GHOST...He did not teach them that He was the Son of the Holy Ghost, but the Son of the Father. He was not born without the aid of man, and that man was God! Doctrines of Salvation by Joseph Fielding Smith, Vol. 1, pg. 18

The fleshly body of Jesus required a Mother as well as a Father. Therefore, the Father and Mother of Jesus, according to the flesh, must have been associated together in the capacity of husband and wife; hence the Virgin Mary must have been, for the time being, the lawful wife of God the Father: we use the term lawful Wife, because it would be blasphemous in the highest degree to say that He overshadowed her or begat the Saviour unlawfully.

It would have been unlawful for any man to have interfered with Mary, who was already espoused to Joseph; for such heinous crime would have subjected both the guilty parties to death, according to the law of Moses. But God having created all men and women, had the most perfect right to overshadow the Virgin Mary in the capacity of a husband, and beget a Son, although she was espoused to another; for the law He gave to govern men and women was not intended to govern Himself, or to prescribe rules for his own conduct. It was also unlawful in Him, after having thus dealt with Mary, to give her to Joseph for time only, or for time and eternity, we are not informed. In as much as God was the first husband to her, it may be that He only gave her to be the wife of Joseph while in this mortal state, and that he intended after the resurrection to again take her as one of his own wives to raise up immortal spirits in eternity. The Seer, pg. 158

Here we see the Mormon teaching that God the Father came down and co-habitated with one of His own *spirit-children*, Mary. Sounds somewhat incestuous. Also, God the Father was already married in heaven (probably to many wives), and He has relations with someone (Mary) who is already betrothed to someone else (Joseph). Sounds rather adulterous. The Bible sets the matter straight in Luke 1:34, 35.

E. JESUS WAS MARRIED WHILE ON EARTH

It will be borne in mind that once on a time, there was a marriage in Cana of Galilee; and on a careful reading of that transaction, it will be discovered that no less a person than Jesus Christ was married on that occasion. If he was never married, his intimacy with Mary and Martha, and the other Mary also whom Jesus loved, must have been highly unbecoming and improper to say the best of it. Journal of Discourses, Orson Hyde, Vol. 4, pg. 259

Isn't it a little strange that Jesus would be INVITED, just like His disciples, to HIS OWN WEDDING? See John 2:1-2. After the miracle of changing the water into wine, Jesus and His mother, brethren, and disciples went down to Capernaum; but no mention was made of His new wife going down with Him, or even staying behind (John 2:11-12)! In fact, there is no mention in scripture whatsoever of a wife of Jesus during his earthly ministry.

Do we not also detect the implication in Orson Hyde's statement that Jesus was also polygamous?

For further information on this Mormon teaching see Journal of Discourses, Vol. 13, pg. 309 and The Seer, pg. 172.

F. JESUS IS A VENGEFUL DESTROYER

According to the Book of Mormon, at Christ's death sixteen cities were destroyed and thousands of people were killed (III Nephi 8).

Chapter Four
SALVATION OR EXALTATION?

In Galatians 1:6-9 the Apostle Paul makes some very serious statements concerning the purity of the gospel that he preached. The souls of men are in the balances as we present God's plan of salvation. What if a warped, diluted, inflated, or otherwise perverted gospel is presented? Only eternity will reveal the damage done by perverters of the gospel.

The Bible gospel is a simple one (I Corinthians 15:1-4), the Mormon gospel, as we shall see, is very complicated and confusing. In fact, the Mormon church does not offer SALVATION from sin, but a complex plan of EXALTATION to *godhood*.

I.   BIBLE PLAN OF SALVATION

The Christian understanding of salvation, as taught in the Bible, is not complicated. In the first place, the Bible teaches that all of mankind has sinned and faces the judgment of God:

All have sinned and come short of the glory of God.

Roman 3:23

The soul that sinneth, it shall die. Ezekiel 18:20

The wicked shall be turned into hell, and all nations that forget God. Psalms 9:17

The Bible also teaches that God has provided a way to forgiveness and eternal life. It is not something we can do. It is something God has already done for us! It can be summed up in one scripture:

For God so loved the world, that He gave His only begotten Son, that whosoever believeth in Him should not perish, but have everlasting life. John 3:16

The Christian believes that it is ONLY through faith in Christ's blood atonement that men can be forgiven of sin and released from its penalties (Colossians 1:14).

For He hath made Him to be sin for us, who knew no sin, that we might be made the righteousness of God in Him. II Corinthians 5:21

The Bible teaches that salvation is a free gift, a

price already paid, unearned by us:

A.   Ephesians 2:8,9 - *not of yourselves: it is the gift of God.*

B.   Galatians 2:21 - *I do not frustrate the grace of God: for if righteousness come by the law, then Christ is dead in vain.*

C.   Galatians 3:24 - *that we might be justified by faith.*

The Bible also teaches that those who receive Christ by faith, and call on Him for salvation are instantly and eternally saved from their sins:

D.   John 1:12 – *as many as received him to them gave he power to become the sons of God.*

E.   Romans 10:13 - *For whosoever shall call upon the name of the Lord shall be saved.*

F.   John 5:24 - *and believeth on him that sent me, hath everlasting life.*

The Bible is also clear on the fact that those who refuse GOD'S PROVISION of salvation will experience eternal damnation: Revelation 20:11-15;

John 3:36; Revelation 14:11. There are only two kinds of people, SAVED and LOST.

II.   MORMON PLAN OF EXALTATION

A.   TWO KINDS OF MORMON SALVATION

Articles two and three of the Articles of Faith, by James Talmage, give a brief look into Mormon doctrine regarding salvation:

Article 2: *We believe that men will be punished for their own sins and not for Adam's transgression.*

Article 3: *We believe that through the Atonement of Christ, all mankind may be saved, by obedience to the Laws and Ordinances of the Gospel.*

Volumes have been written by Mormons on their views of salvation. Perhaps the most accurate and widely accepted work in this area is the Articles of Faith. In his work, Talmage goes into great detail taking over 40 pages of text, and over 10 pages of notes to cover the aforementioned two articles of faith. The summation of these words is the LDS position that there are actually two levels of salvation:

1. LEVEL ONE - GENERAL SALVATION
Talmage explains in this way:

The extent of the atonement is universal, applying alike to all descendants of Adam. Even the unbeliever, the heathen and the child who dies before reaching the years of discretion all are redeemed by the Saviour's self-sacrifice from the individual consequences of the fall. Articles of Faith, pg. 85

In other words, Christ's death upon the cross brought a general salvation for all men, which is later explained as a resurrection in order to be judged for our works.

2. LEVEL TWO - INDIVIDUAL SALVATION OR EXALTATION

Exaltation is given to those only who by righteous effort have won a claim to God's merciful liberality...Of the Saved, not all will be exalted to the higher glories. No one can be admitted to any order of glory, in short, no soul can be saved until justice has been satisfied for violated law...In the Kingdom of God there are numerous degrees or graduations provided for those who are worthy of them. Articles of Faith, pg. 91

The essence of Talmage's words express the basic Mormon doctrine that Christ's atonement places all mankind at a judgment table where we shall be reviewed for our righteousness and our works, or obedience to *the laws and ordinances of the gospel*.

The Mormon concept is, depending upon their worthiness, men have access to three different kingdoms, or levels of glory:

The Celestial Glory - There are some who have striven to obey all the divine commandments, who have accepted the testimony of Christ, obeyed 'the laws and ordinances of the Gospel'....they are admitted to the glorified company, crowned with exaltation in the celestial kingdom.

The Terrestrial Glory - We read of others who receive glory of a secondary order, differing from the highest....These are they who, though honorable, failed to comply with the requirements for exaltation, were blinded by the craftiness of men and unable to receive and obey the higher laws of God. They proved 'not valiant in the testimony of Jesus,' and therefore are not entitled to the fullness of glory.

The Telestial Glory - There is another grade, differing from the higher orders....this is for those who received not the testimony of Christ, but who, nevertheless, did not deny the Holy Spirit; who have led lives exempting them from the heaviest punishment, yet whose redemption will be delayed until the last resurrection. Then there are those who have lost all claim upon the immediate mercy of God, whose deeds have numbered them with Perdition and his angels. Articles of Faith, pg. 91-93

Note that hell (Perdition) is added as an afterthought to the last kingdom (Telestial). This three-tiered heaven comes from a twisted exegesis of I Corinthians 15:38-44 with a coined Mormon word added (Telestial). More will be said on this in the next chapter.

B. A GOSPEL OF WORKS

Article four of the Articles of Faith states:

We believe that the first principles and ordinances of the Gospel are: first, Faith in the Lord Jesus Christ; second, Repentance; third, Baptism by immersion for the remission of sins; fourth, Laying on of hands for the gift of the Holy Ghost.

A thirty-one page booklet entitled *The Plan of Salvation* by the Mormon church states:

We consider that enough has been said to establish the principles we have advanced, and we will call upon all to whom these words shall come to exercise faith in the gospel of Jesus Christ, to repent of their sins, to be baptized for the remission of them, to receive the laying on of hands for the gift of the Holy Ghost, and then to serve the God of Israel with all their might, mind and strength.

These last two quotes sound like something out of a theological horror chamber. Bible salvation is attacked and substituted with an elaborate system of works. The following Bible texts easily dismiss these Mormon notions:

But to him that worketh not, but believeth on him that justifieth the ungodly, his faith is counted for righteousness. Romans 4:5

For by grace are ye saved through faith; and that not of yourselves: it is the gift of God: Not of works, lest any man should boast. Ephesians 2:8,9

Note the emphasis laid upon the Mormon church

organization and administration in salvation:

The President of the Church of Jesus Christ of Latter-day Saints holds the keys of salvation for all men now living because he is the only one by whose authorization the sealing power of the priesthood can be used to seal up men to salvation and exaltation in the kingdom of God. Mormon Doctrine, by Bruce R. McConkie, pg. 411

John 14:6 gives the words of our Lord Jesus Christ himself in reply to such foolishness:

Jesus saith unto him, I am the way, the truth, and the life: no man cometh unto the Father, but by me. John 14:6

See also II Nephi 2:22-27 in the Book of Mormon to understand the peculiar idea Joseph Smith had that Adam *fell upward.* Joseph Smith's strange idea about pre-existence and the need to obtain a body to effect salvation led to this error. A casual reading of I Corinthians 15:45-48 shows the physical comes first, then the spiritual, and NOT the other way around as Joseph Smith taught.

C. MORMON DOCTRINE OF BLOOD ATONEMENT

On February 8, 1857, Mormon church president Brigham Young said the following in a discourse given at the Tabernacle in Salt Lake City, Utah:

....suppose that he is overtaken in a gross fault, that he has committed a sin that he knows will deprive him of that exaltation which he desires, and that he cannot attain to it without the shedding of his blood, and also knows that by having his blood shed he will atone for that sin, and be saved and exalted with the Gods, is there a man or woman in this house but would say 'shed my blood that I may be saved and exalted with the Gods?'

All mankind love themselves and let these principles be known by an individual, and he would be glad to have his blood shed. That would be loving themselves, even unto an eternal exaltation. Will you love your brothers or sisters likewise, when they have committed a sin that cannot be atoned for without the shedding of their blood? Will you love that man or woman well enough to shed their blood? Journal of Discourses, Vol. 4, pg. 219

The issue of whether or not any modern Mormons

believe in suicide for salvation is not our point here. The issue is that the complete work of Christ on the cross is minimized to suggest that there is a sin that HIS precious blood could NOT atone for. The nature of this blasphemy is simply directed against the complete and finished work of Christ on the cross.

It is the nature of Satan's program to belittle the fullness of God's salvation presented to mankind in the person of Jesus Christ. The doctrine of *Blood Atonement* as taught by Brigham Young is one example of Satan's success in using a church that claims to be Christian for the advancement of his own lies.

But if we walk in the light, as He is in the light, we have fellowship one with another, and the blood of Jesus Christ His Son cleanseth us from ALL SIN. I John 1:7

D. MORMONISM SEEKS EXALTATION, NOT SALVATION

Much was said on this subject in our second chapter on the nature of the Godhead. But consider the following quotes in the context of salvation:

Thus all men who ascend to the glorious state of Godhood can do so only by one method - by obedience to all the principles and ordinances of the Gospel of Jesus Christ...If to obtain eternal life means to enjoy the same type of life that God lives and to experience similar experiences, then those people who receive it to the fullest degree shall actually be Gods. The Gospel Through the Ages, Milton R. Hunter, pg. 115-117

Here, then, is eternal life, to know the only wise and true God; and you have got to learn how to be Gods yourselves, and to be kings and priests to God, the same as all Gods have done before you, namely, by going from one small degree to another, and from a small capacity to a great one; from grace to grace, from exaltation to exaltation, until you attain to the resurrection of the dead, and are able to dwell in everlasting burnings, and to sit in glory, as do those who sit enthroned in everlasting power. Teachings of the Prophet Joseph Smith, by Joseph Fielding Smith, pg. 346, 347

We can easily see that the knowledgeable Mormon is interested in doing what Eve desired in Genesis 3, and is not very concerned about being freed from the damning results of what took place in Genesis 3! THE MORMON PROSPECT FOR SALVATION MUST BE MADE TO SEE THAT HE IS A HELL-BOUND SINNER before any talk of Christ saving him will be of any real value.

For the Son of man is come to seek and to save that WHICH WAS LOST. Luke 19:10

Chapter Five
WHERE DO THE DEAD GO?

Some modern religions scoff at the idea of an afterlife. They believe *once dead, always dead*; others contend that we're reincarnated animals (of whatever sort).

Mormonism has successfully combined the pagan concept of man's pre-existence with an ELABORATE PERVERSION of the Bible's teaching on the afterlife.

I. <u>BIBLE VIEW OF THE AFTERLIFE</u>

Without going into detail on the Christian's rewards, the post-resurrection situation is VERY SIMPLE FOR THE SAVED; death allows the release of the soul and spirit to be in the IMMEDIATE presence of God in the third heaven.

We are confident, I say, and willing rather to be absent from the body, and to be present with the Lord. II Corinthians 5:8

And they stoned Stephen, calling upon God, and saying, Lord Jesus, receive my spirit. And he kneeled down, and cried with a loud voice, Lord, lay not this sin to their charge. And when he had said this, he fell asleep. Acts 7:59,60

The believer's body (which is said to *sleep*) awaits a glorified resurrection to be united with the soul and the spirit.

But I would not have you to be ignorant, brethren, concerning them which are asleep, that ye sorrow not, even as others which have no hope. For if we believe that Jesus died and rose again, even so them also which sleep in Jesus will God bring with him. For this we say unto you by the word of the Lord, that we which are alive and remain unto the coming of the Lord shall not prevent them which are asleep. For the Lord himself shall descend from heaven with a shout, with the voice of the archangel and with the trump of God: and the dead in Christ shall rise first: Then we which are alive and remain shall be caught up together with them in the clouds, to meet the Lord in the air: and so shall we ever be with the Lord. Wherefore comfort one another with these words. I Thessalonians 4:13-18

FOR THE LOST we see a very different scenario. Those who die without Christ as their Savior go to a place of conscious punishment called Hell. As their dead body decays in the grave, their soul and spirit suffer the torments of the damned.

The wicked shall be turned into hell, and all the nations that forget God. Psalms 9:17

And the smoke of their torment ascendeth up for ever and ever: and they have no rest day nor night, who worship the beast and his image, and whosoever receiveth the mark of his name. Revelation 14:11

And it came to pass, that the beggar died, and was carried by the angels into Abraham's bosom: the rich man also died, and was buried; And in hell he lift up his eyes being in torments, and seeth Abraham afar off, and Lazarus in his bosom. And he cried and said, Father Abraham have mercy on me, and send Lazarus, that he may dip the tip of his finger in water, and cool my tongue; for I am tormented in this flame. Luke 16:22-24

The lost will eventually be judged at the Great White Throne Judgment (after the 1,000 year reign of Christ on the earth), and be cast into a lake of fire for all eternity (body, soul, and spirit together) after this last resurrection of damnation:

And I saw a great white throne, and him that sat on it, from whose face the earth and the heaven fled away; and there was found no place for them. And I saw the dead, small and great, stand before God; and another book was opened, which is the book of life: and the dead were judged out of those things which were written in the books, according to their works. And the sea gave up the dead which were in them: and they were judged every man according to their works. And death and hell were cast into the lake of fire. This is the second death. And whosoever was not found written in the book of life was cast into the lake of fire. Revelation 20:11-15

II. MORMON VIEW OF THE AFTERLIFE

A. PRE-EXISTENCE

Before we discuss the afterlife, we must understand the Mormon concept of pre-existence. We will first give a brief summary of the Mormon teaching before we give any direct quotes.

We have always existed. FIRST, we were eternal intelligences. This is the first part of our pre-existence. Our Heavenly Father (at least for this earth) cohabitated with one or more *heavenly mothers* which resulted in spirit beings created over a period of time (at least for this earth). In some way, these intelligences became spirits. As spirits, they had to stay in heaven until bodies were created for them on this earth.

THE FIRST OF THESE SPIRITS was Jesus. The second was Lucifer. They were given an opportunity by the Father to present a plan of salvation to redeem men and women on the earth. Lucifer's plan was to redeem everyone. But Jesus had a plan to redeem only those who wanted it, thus preserving their free agency. Jesus' plan was accepted, and Lucifer became very upset. He rebelled and became Satan. A third of the spirit-children sided with him. They rebelled and were cast out of heaven becoming the devil and his angels.

THE FIRST FAVORED PEOPLE WITH BODIES ON THE EARTH were Adam and Eve. They were placed in the Garden of Eden by the Father, and given two *contradictory commands, Be fruitful and multiply*...Genesis 1:28, and *but of the tree of the knowledge of good and evil, thou shalt not eat of it: for in that day that thou eatest thereof thou shalt surely die.* Genesis 2:17. Knowing that they could not keep the first command until they broke the second, they *wisely* chose to fall in the *right direction* by breaking the second. Once this was done they were able to have children with bodies of flesh and bone just like their heavenly parents (i.e. the Father and Mother(s), except these were not glorified resurrection bodies. The children's bodies would provide homes for spirits created in the pre-existence. It was essential they get bodies, because without them, no one could progress to *become a God*, just like their Heavenly Father and Heavenly Mother(s) did.

IN THIS LIFE men are on probation. In the next, depending on what they did, all men will go to one of three degrees of glory, better than what we have here (except for a relatively few *sons of perdition*). Even those who died without hearing the gospel can be saved with the help of the living (i.e. *baptism for the dead* which we'll look at in the next chapter).

In the previous four chapters, we have documented and biblically refuted most of the above mentioned Mormon concepts. The following will demonstrate the Mormon concept of pre-existence.

Let us then refer to the word of the Lord, which is the end of the argument, and see what the teachings of the Great Creator of all are.

Speaking to Job, one of the most ancient writers of the Bible he says: 'Who is this that darkeneth counsel by words without knowledge? Gird up now thy loins like a man: for I will demand of thee, and answer thou me. Where wast thou when I laid the foundations of the earth?....When the morning stars sang together, and all the sons of God shouted for joy'.

Job certainly must have been somewhere when the 'foundations of the earth were laid.' or why the question?

Again, we find that the apostles must have had some conception of pre-existence, judging from their question to Jesus: 'Master, who did sin, this man, or his parents, that he was born blind.'

It is evident that the question was not a doubtful one in the minds of the apostles as to whether a man could sin previous to his existence in the flesh, but as to whether this particular man had sinned or not. A thirty-one page booklet entitled *The Plan of Salvation* by the Mormon church, pg. 2-4

The scriptural wresting (II Peter 3:16) and tortured

logic demonstrated above shows a complete lack of understanding of the simplest Bible concepts. For example, in the first incident cited (Job 38), God is proving to Job that He is superior to man because man DID NOT EXIST when God was creating, therefore he has no right to judge God's ways. A casual reading of the Book of Job will easily yield this much understanding.

In the Second example (taken from John 9) the Mormon authors of the booklet are injecting their presupposition in to the narrative by ASSUMING the apostles were referring to a *previous existence*. The plain sense of the text, without the Mormon mental gymnastics demonstrated, reveals a simple question regarding some possible sin the man or his parents could have committed to cause the man's blindness. The sin would have been committed in THIS LIFE. Roughly fifty percent of the world's blindness is a direct result of venereal disease, with the parents passing the handicap on to the next generation.

It is obvious that these concepts are not biblical at all. In fact, it sounds more like a theological pipe dream when compared with the Bible. Hebrews 9:27 destroys all concepts of reincarnation, as well as the Mormon *cycle of life*.

And as it is appointed unto men once to die, but after this the judgment.

B.   THREE DEGREES OF GLORY

This subject was dealt with in our last chapter (Chapter Four). For the purpose of this chapter, let's examine the Mormon *proof text* for their three degrees of glory.

There are also celestial bodies, and bodies terrestrial: but the glory of the celestial is one, and the glory of the terrestrial is another. There is one glory of the sun, and another glory of the moon, and another glory of the stars: for one star differeth from another star in glory.   I Corinthians 15:40,41

Mormons have great difficulty with this passage.

A breakdown of the Mormon teaching of the three levels of glory is as follows:

1. Celestial Kingdom is reserved for those obedient members of the Melchizekek Priesthood, who shall, after the fashion of our God, become Gods themselves, with their worthy wives.

2.   Terrestrial Kingdom is a secondary degree set

aside for those who, though honorable, failed to comply with the requirements for exaltation, or for those who proved not valiant in the testimony of Jesus Christ.

3.   Telestial Kingdom is the lowest of the three. It is reserved for those who had no testimony of Christ or the gospel.

Is this what I Corinthians 15 is really teaching? Let's first consider terminology:

Telestial - a coined Mormon word.

Terrestrial - is by definition *earthly*.

Celestial - is by definition *heavenly*.

The Bible interpretation of this passage is that man is on earth with a *terrestrial body* and will be resurrected with a *celestial body*. This passage is talking about states of our bodies, not *heavens*. NOTICE WHAT THE BIBLE REALLY TEACHES ABOUT THE THREE HEAVENS:

1. The first heaven is the earth and its atmosphere:

In the six hundredth year of Noah's life, in the second month, the seventeenth day of the month, the same day were all the foundations of the great deep broken up, and the windows of heaven were opened. Genesis 7:11

And I will appoint over them four kinds, saith the Lord: the sword to slay, and the dogs to tear, and the fowls of the heaven, and the beasts of the earth, to devour and destroy. Jeremiah 15:3

And then shall appear the sign of the Son of man in heaven: and then shall all the tribes of the earth mourn, and they shall see the Son of man coming in the clouds of heaven with power and great glory. Matthew 24:30

2. The second heaven is planetary.

And God said, Let there be lights in the firmament of the heaven to divide the day from the night; and let them be for signs, and for seasons, and for days and years: And let them be for lights in the firmament of heaven to give light upon the earth: and it was so. Genesis 1:14,15

The heavens declare the glory of God; and the firmament sheweth his handywork. Psalms 19:1

3. The third heaven is where God sits on His throne.

But will God indeed dwell on the earth? behold, the heaven and heaven of heavens cannot contain thee; how much less this house that I have builded?....And hearken thou to the supplication of thy servant, and of thy people Israel, when they shall pray toward this place: and hear thou in heaven thy dwelling place: and when thou hearest forgive. I Kings 8:27, 30

After this manner therefore pray ye: Our Father which art in heaven, Hallowed be thy name. Matthew 6:9

I knew a man in Christ above fourteen years ago, (whether in the body, I cannot tell; or whether out of the body, I cannot tell: God knoweth;) such an one caught up to the third heaven. II Corinthians 12:2

C. SONS OF PERDITION

Bruce R. McConkie explains the concept of sons of perdition.

Lucifer is Perdition. He became such by open

rebellion against the truth, a rebellion in the face of light and knowledge...In rebellion with him were one-third of the spirit hosts of heaven. These all were thus followers (or in other words, sons of perdition). They were denied bodies, were cast out onto the earth, and thus came the devil and his angels - a great host of sons of perdition.

Those in this life who gain a perfect knowledge of the divinity of the gospel cause, a knowledge that comes only by revelation from the Holy Ghost, and who then link themselves with Lucifer and come out in open rebellion, also become sons of perdition. Their destiny, following their resurrection is to be cast out with the devil and his angels, to inherit the same kingdom in a state where 'their worm dieth not, and the fire is not quenched'. Doctrine and Covenants 76:32-49; 29:27-30, Mormon Doctrine, by Bruce R. McConkie, pg, 746

Joseph Fielding Smith tells of the FEW who will be sons of perdition.

Before a man can sink to this bitterness of soul, he must first know and understand the truth with a clearness of vision wherein there is no doubt...How fortunate it is that in the mercy of God there will be comparatively few who will partake of this awful misery and eternal darkness. Doctrines of Salvation by Joseph Fielding Smith, Vol. 1, pg. 49.

A casual reading of scripture will easily demonstrate the OPPOSITE of Mormon teaching on the percentages that are likely to inhabit Hell (i.e. *Perdition*).

Enter ye in at the strait gate: for wide is the gate, and broad is the way, that leadeth to destruction, and MANY there be which go in thereat: Because strait is the gate, and narrow is the way, which leadeth unto life, and FEW there be that find it. Beware of false prophets, which come to you in sheep's clothing, but inwardly they are ravening wolves. Matthew 7:13-15

CHAPTER SIX
BAPTISM FOR THE DEAD

The Mormon church owns and operates an elaborate library for genealogical research. This library, located across the street from the Mormon temple in Salt Lake City, Utah, is the largest of its kind anywhere in the world.

One might ask, *Why go to such expense and trouble just to learn about your family tree?* The answer lies in the Mormon doctrine of BAPTISM FOR THE DEAD with its attendant after-death, second chance salvation by proxy.

I. BIBLE VIEW OF THE AFTERLIFE - NO SECOND CHANCE

A casual reading of the Bible will easily yield the following truths:

A. There is one life, death and judgment.

And as it is appointed unto men once to die, but after this the judgment. Hebrews 9:27

B. The spiritual condition a soul dies in is the

condition that soul remains in for eternity.

I said therefore unto you, that ye shall die in your sins; for if ye believe not that I am he, ye shall die in your sins. John 8:24

He that is unjust, let him be unjust still: and he which is filthy, let him be filthy still: and he that is righteous, let him be righteous still: and he that is holy, let him be holy still. Revelation 22:11

C. The living cannot effect the state of the dead by proxy, neither can the dead effect the state of the living.

None of them can by any means redeem his brother, nor give to God a ransom for him: (For the redemption of their soul is precious, and it ceaseth for ever:) Psalms 49:7,8

And it came to pass, that the beggar died, and was carried by the angels into Abraham's bosom: the rich man also died, and was buried; And in hell he lift up his eyes being in torments, and seeth Abraham afar off, and Lazarus in his bosom. And he cried and said, Father Abraham have mercy on me, and send Lazarus, that he may dip the tip of his finger in water, and cool my tongue; for I am tormented in this flame. But Abraham said, Son remember that thou in thy lifetime receivest thy good things, and likewise Lazarus evil things: but now he is comforted, and thou art tormented. And beside all this, between us and you there is a great gulf fixed: so that they which would pass from hence to you cannot; neither can they pass to us, that would come from thence. Then he said, I pray thee therefore, father, that thou wouldest send him to my father's house: For I have five brethren; that he may testify unto them, lest they also come into this place of torment. Abraham saith unto him, They have Moses and the prophets; let them hear them. And he said, Nay, father Abraham: but if one went unto them from the dead, they will repent. And he said unto him, If they hear not Moses and the prophets, neither will they be persuaded, though one rose from the dead. Luke 16:22-31

D. Genealogical research outside of the Bible itself, for spiritual purposes, is NOT a desirable thing for the Christian.

Neither give heed to fables and endless genealogies, which minister questions, rather than godly edifying which is in faith: so do.

I Timothy 1:4

But avoid foolish questions, and genealogies, and contentions, and strivings about the law; for they are unprofitable and vain. Titus 3:9

The scriptures we've quoted are only a small sampling of what becomes OBVIOUS when someone has only a minimal working knowledge of the Bible. The Mormon church must go OUTSIDE OF THE BIBLE and CONTRADICT THE BIBLE in order to *prove* it's case concerning baptism for the dead.

II. <u>MORMON BAPTISM FOR THE DEAD</u>

And now, my dearly beloved brethren and sisters, let me assure you that these are principles in relation to the dead and the living that cannot be lightly passed over, as pertaining to our salvation. For their salvation is necessary and essential to our salvation, as Paul says concerning the fathers - that they without us cannot be made perfect - neither can we without our dead be made perfect....Let us, therefore, as a church and a people, and as Latterday Saints, offer unto the Lord an offering in righteousness; and let us present in his holy temple, when it is finished, a book containing the records of

our dead, which shall be worthy of all acceptation.
Doctrine and Covenants, Sec. 128:15,24b

The reason for this emphasis on genealogical research is that Mormons believe in a second chance salvation where those who have died without a chance to hear the gospel may be baptized by proxy via a living member of the Mormon church.

Joseph Fielding Smith stated:

Divisions in the Spirit World. All spirits of men after death return to the spirit world. There, as I understand it, the righteous - meaning those who have been baptized and who have been faithful - are gathered in one part and all the others in another part of the spirit world. This seems to be true from the vision given to President Joseph F. Smith and found in Gospel Doctrine. What the Lord really said to the thief was that he would be with him in the world of spirits and there he would be taught the truth, as this seemed to be his desire while upon the cross. Doctrines of Salvation by Joseph Fielding Smith, Vol. 2, pg. 230

Bruce R. McConkie stated:

Salvation for the Dead, Spirit Prison. By spirit world is meant the abiding place of disembodied spirits.....This world is divided into two parts: paradise which is the abode of the righteous, and hell which is the abode of the wicked. (Alma 40:11-14).....when the wicked spirits repent, they leave their prison-hell and join the righteous in paradise. Mormon Doctrine, by Bruce R. McConkie, pg. 761, 762

.....the righteous spirits in paradise have been commissioned to carry the message of salvation to the wicked spirits in hell. Mormon Doctrine, by Bruce R. McConkie, pg. 755

Those who accept Mormonism in the Spirit Prison must have a mortal do their baptism and temple ordinances for them in order to enter the Celestial Kingdom. Thus, today we have Mormons doing what they believe will be vicarious work for the dead in their temples.

WRESTING THE SCRIPTURES

In II Peter 3:16, 17 we are warned about those who misuse the Bible by wresting the scriptures. To wrest a text of scripture is to twist and wrestle it out of context, forcing it into one's own private interpretation, regardless of what the rest of the Bible clearly teaches on the same subject.

As also in all his epistles, speaking in them of these things; in which are some things hard to be understood, which they that are unlearned and unstable wrest, as they do also the other scriptures, unto their own destruction. Ye therefore, beloved, seeing ye know these things before, beware lest ye also, being led away with the error of the wicked, fall from your own steadfastness. II Peter 3:16, 17

It is not unusual to find a cultist (of whatever sort) basing an entire false doctrine upon one phrase of one difficult, or obscure passage of scripture. The interpretation will always run contrary to as many as three hundred clear scripture texts on the same subject that teach exactly the opposite of what the self-made theologian is trying to prove. Such is the case with the Mormon teaching on *baptism for the dead*, as extracted from I Corinthians 15:29

Else what shall they do which are baptized for the dead, if the dead rise not at all? why are they then baptized for the dead? I Corinthians 15:29

It would be foolish to say that this scripture was easy to understand. Many theologians have offered their interpretation of it and have come to differing conclusions. The question we need to ask is, *Does it teach that we can be baptized for dead people by proxy*?

A careful examination will show that it says *they do,* not *we do*. If Paul had been practicing baptism for the dead, he would have said *we,* not *they*. It is apparent then that Paul was not practicing it, but (if anyone was practicing it) the very people who taught that there was no resurrection were teaching that someone who had died could be baptized by proxy. Paul would be pointing out how foolish such a practice was.

It is also apparent that one is baptized BECAUSE of death. If we didn't ever die, we wouldn't need to be baptized at all. Baptism pictures not only a death, but a resurrection. Since these folks didn't believe in the resurrection, Paul points out that we are really baptized BECAUSE of death. If there is no resurrection from death, why be baptized? As believers, we died and rose with Christ, thus we practice scriptural baptism.

Notice this same use of the word *for* (meaning *because of*) in the following verses.

For I delivered unto you first of all that which I also received, how that Christ died for our sins according to the scriptures. I Corinthians 15:3

But God commendeth his love toward us, in that, while we were yet sinners, Christ died for us. Romans 5:8

In the above quoted verses it is obvious that Christ died **BECAUSE** WE ARE SINNERS, NOT to give us the opportunity to BECOME SINNERS. The word *for* carries the same idea in I Corinthians 15:29.

What is also interesting is that the Book of Mormon itself negates the Mormon practice of baptism for the dead.

And, in fine, wo unto all those who died in their sins; for they shall return to God, and behold his face, and remain in their sins. 2 Nephi 9:38

For behold, this life is the time for men to prepare to meet God; yea, behold the day of this life is the day for men to perform their labors. And now, as I said unto you before, as ye have had so many witnesses, therefore, I beseech of you that ye do not procrastinate the day of your repentance until the end; for after this day of life, which is given us to prepare for eternity, behold, if we do not improve our time while in this life, then cometh the night of darkness wherein there can be no labor performed. Ye cannot say, when ye are brought to that awful crisis, that I will repent, that I will return to my God. Nay, ye cannot say this; for that same spirit which doth possess your bodies at the time that ye go out of this life, that same spirit will have power to possess your body in that eternal world. For behold, if ye have procrastinated the day of your repentance even until death, behold, ye have become subjected to the spirit of the devil, and he doth seal you his; therefore, the Spirit of the Lord hath withdrawn from you, and hath no place in you, and the devil hath all power over you; and this is the final state of the wicked. Alma 34:32-35

The Mormon position that I Corinthian 15:29 refers to proxy baptism for the dead as they practice it, for the reasons they practice it, rests upon five suppositions:

A. Baptism saves (it doesn't).

B. There is second-chance salvation (there isn't).

C. Paul was referring to Christians who were

doing the baptisms (notice that Paul says *they* not *we* in this verse).

D. Being concerned with genealogies is a good thing (it isn't, biblically speaking - I Timothy 1:4; Titus 3:9). Only one genealogy could be said to be significant for Christians today, and that is the one for *the Lion of the Tribe of Judah, the Root of David* (Revelation 5:5), that is, for the Lord Jesus Christ.

E. Paul meant baptism for the dead in exactly the same way that the Mormon church does (impossible, in view of the preceding).

III.   THE GREATEST COMMANDMENT?

Joseph Smith stated

The greatest responsibility in this world that God has laid upon us, is to seek after our dead. Times and Seasons, Vol. 5, pg. 616

It seems strange that if doing temple work for the dead is our *GREATEST RESPONSIBILITY* that JESUS NEVER MENTIONED IT!

Jesus was once asked by one of the scribes

Which is the first commandment of all? And Jesus answered him, The first of all the commandments is, Hear O Israel; the Lord our God is one Lord: And thou shalt love the Lord thy God with all thy heart, and with all thy soul, and with all thy mind, and with all thy strength: this is the FIRST COMMANDMENT. And the second is like, namely this, Thou shalt love thy neighbor as thyself. There is none other COMMANDMENT GREATER than these. Mark 12:28-31

Some Mormons boast of having been baptized as many as four hundred times for the sake of those that have died without the gospel.

A thirty-one page booklet entitled *The Plan of Salvation* by the Mormon church states

We have here an explanation as to how their prison doors may be opened and they set free: by the ordinance of the gospel through the baptism for the dead. Those that are in the flesh do vicarious work for their dead and become 'saviors upon Mount Zion.'

IV. <u>CONCLUSION</u>

The Bible makes it clear that we have only one

life in which to choose Christ (this present life), and only WE can make that decision for ourselves - CHOOSE NOW TO TRUST JESUS CHRIST AS YOUR PERSONAL SAVIOUR.

And as Moses lifted up the serpent in the wilderness, even so must the Son of man be lifted up: That whosoever believeth in him should not perish, but have eternal life. For God so love the world, that he gave his only begotten Son, that whosoever believeth in him should not perish, but have everlasting life. For God sent not his Son into the world to condemn the world; but that the world through him might be saved. He that believeth on him is not condemned; but he that believeth not is condemned already, because he hath not believed in the name of the only begotten Son of God. And this is the condemnation, that light is come into the world, and men loved darkness rather than light, because their deeds were evil. For every one that doeth evil hateth the light, neither cometh to the light, lest his deeds should be reproved. But he that doeth truth cometh to the light, that his deeds may be made manifest, that they are wrought in God. John 3:14-21

CHAPTER SEVEN
JOSEPH SMITH

As we have seen in previous chapters, Mormonism does not hold the Bible as its final authority. Mormonism stands or falls on the testimony of Joseph Smith. This will be easy to demonstrate as we examine the claims of Joseph Smith. In fact, after examining the evidence (statements made by Joseph Smith himself, and what his followers have said about him over the years), this writer is convinced that Joseph Smith is to Mormonism what the Lord Jesus Christ is to Bible Christianity. In other words, for all practical purposes, Joseph Smith is MORMONISM'S CHRIST!

I.   THE CULT MENTALITY

A cult is a system of religious worship built around, or centered in, a devoted attachment to, or an EXTRAVAGANT ADMIRATION OF A PERSON.

By this definition, Mormonism is a cult, because, as we shall see, Mormons have an extravagant admiration for Joseph Smith. We will also observe that Joseph Smith had an inflated opinion of himself.

Admittedly the label *cult* could be subjectively attached to most religions by those who disagree with that religion's doctrine. Judaism would view Christianity as a cult, because in their view, Christians have a devoted attachment to, and an extravagant admiration for the Lord Jesus Christ. Orthodox Jews do not believe Him to be God.

Consider the claims of Christ's deity as found in the Bible:

Jesus saith unto him, I am the way, the truth, and the life: no man cometh unto the Father, but by me. John 14:6

Neither is there salvation in any other: for there is none other name under heaven given among men, whereby we must be saved. Acts 4:12

And without controversy great is the mystery of godliness: God was manifest in the flesh, justified in the Spirit, seen of angels, preached unto the Gentiles, believed on in the world, received up into glory. I Timothy 3:16

But unto the Son he saith, Thy throne, O God is for ever and ever: a sceptre of righteousness is the sceptre of thy kingdom. Hebrews 1:8

The issue here is a simple one - either Jesus Christ IS who the Bible says He is, and Christians worship the true God, or Bible-believing Christians have an unwarranted and *extravagant admiration* for Jesus Christ, making them members of a cult. The issue here is one of ABSOLUTE TRUTH. Who is telling the truth?

Therefore, to avoid a subjective labeling of Mormonism as a cult, we must either prove the claims of the man-worshippers to be false, and label them cultists (Joseph Smith/Mormons), or find them to be true and acknowledge them so.

EXTRAVAGANT CLAIMS

By their own teachings, Mormons prove that the foundation of their religion is not faith in Jesus Christ, but faith in the mission of Joseph Smith. To demonstrate this statement, we will quote from the writings of Mormonism itself.

Joseph Smith stated

But I am learned, and know more than all the world put together. Teachings of the Prophet Joseph Smith, by Joseph Fielding Smith, pg. 350

THE DIVINE MISSION OF JOSEPH SMITH. CHURCH STANDS OR FALLS WITH JOSEPH SMITH.

Mormonism, as it is called, must stand or fall on the story of Joseph Smith. He was either a prophet of God, divinely called, properly appointed and commissioned, or he was one of the biggest frauds this world has ever seen. There is no middle ground.

NO SALVATION WITHOUT ACCEPTING JOSEPH SMITH.

If Joseph Smith was verily a prophet, and if he told the truth when he said that he stood in the presence of angels sent from the Lord, and obtained keys of authority, and the commandment to organize the Church of Jesus Christ once again on the earth, then this knowledge is of the most vital importance to the entire world. No man can reject that testimony without incurring the most dreadful consequences, for he cannot enter the kingdom of God. It is, therefore, the duty of every man to investigate that he may weigh this matter carefully and know the truth. Doctrines of Salvation by Joseph Fielding Smith, Vol. 1 pg. 188-190

Joseph Smith, the Prophet and Seer of the Lord, has done more, save Jesus only, for the salvation of men in this world, than any other man that ever lived in it. Doctrine and Covenants, 135:3

It is easy to see that Mormonism is not the preaching of the gospel of Jesus Christ, but is rather the glorification of the message and person of a man, Joseph Smith. That message is in total rejection of the salvation provided for us through Jesus Christ.

II. THE FALSE PROPHET

A. OTHER GODS

A true prophet does not turn people to another god. See chapter two in our series to find that Joseph Smith preached faith in a corruptible god/gods.

If there arise among you a prophet, or a dreamer of dreams, and giveth thee a sign or a wonder, And the sign or the wonder come to pass, whereof he spake unto thee, saying, Let us go after other gods, which thou hast not known, and let us serve them; Thou shalt not hearken unto the words of that prophet, or that dreamer of dreams: for the Lord your God proveth you, to know whether ye love the Lord your God with all your heart and with all your soul. Deuteronomy 13:1-3

B.   BIBLE REVISION

Joseph Smith taught altered spiritual truths in his *inspired version* of the Bible by changing God's Holy Word to suit his own understanding.   For example, Romans 4:5 in his *inspired version* says that ungodly men cannot be saved.   Compare the text from God's word (King James Version, 1611) with Joseph Smith's revision.   The teachings are the OPPOSITE OF EACH OTHER.

But to him that worketh not, but believeth on him that justifieth the ungodly, his faith is counted for righteousness.   Romans 4:5, King James Version, 1611

But to him that seeketh not to be justified by the law of works, but believeth on him who justifieth not the ungodly, his faith is counted for righteousness.   Romans 4:5 Joseph Smith's *inspired version*

Note the addition of the word *not* before *the ungodly* by Joseph Smith, thus changing the meaning of the text entirely.

The Bible teaches that God will justify an ungodly man when he comes to Him for forgiveness.

For when we were yet without strength, in due time Christ died for the ungodly. For scarcely for a righteous man will one die: yet peradventure for a good man some would even dare to die. But God commendeth his love toward us, in that, while we were yet sinners, Christ died for us. Much more then, being now justified by his blood, we shall be saved from wrath through him. Romans 5:6-9

In Joseph Smith's *inspired version* of the Bible, Satan reveals himself to be Joseph Smith's God. Matthew 4:1 by Joseph Smith reads

Then Jesus was led up of the Spirit, into the wilderness, to be with God.

The word of God, the Holy Bible states in Matthew 4:1

Then was Jesus led up of the spirit into the

wilderness to be tempted of the devil. King James Version, 1611

Satan signed Joseph Smith's *inspired version* of the Bible as his own.

The Bible teaches us

To the law and to the testimony: if they speak not according to this word, it is because there is no light in them. Isaiah 8:20

C. FALSE PROPHECIES

A real prophet does not give prophecy that fails to come true. Joseph Smith predicted many things which never happened.

The following are only a few of the many prophecies Joseph Smith gave during his lifetime that NEVER CAME TO PASS:

1. That the people of Missouri were to be destroyed *not many years* from 1834 - Doctrine & Covenants 105:13-15

Therefore it is expedient in me that mine elders should wait for a little season, for the redemption of

Zion. For, behold, I do not require at their hands to fight the battles of Zion; for, as I said in a former commandment, even so will I fulfil - I will fight your battles. Behold, the destroyer I have sent forth to destroy and lay wast mine enemies; and not many years hence they shall not be left to pollute mine heritage, and to blaspheme my name upon the lands which I have consecrated for the gathering together of my saints. Doctrine & Covenants 105:13-15

2. Joseph Smith's enemies were to be swept away *not many years* from 1839 - Doctrine and Covenants 121:5-15

Let thine anger be kindled against our enemies; and, in the fury of thine heart, with thy sword avenge us of our wrongs. Remember thy suffering saints, O our God; and thy servants will rejoice in thy name forever. My son, peace be unto thy soul; thine adversity and thine afflictions shall be but a small moment; And then, if thou endure it well, God shall exalt thee on high; thou shalt triumph over all thy foes. Thy friends do stand by thee, and they shall hail thee again with warm hearts and friendly hands.

Thou art not yet as Job; thy friends do not contend

against thee, neither charge thee with transgression, as they did Job. And they who do charge thee with transgression, their hope shall be blasted, and their prospects shall melt away as the hoar frost melteth before the burning rays of the rising sun; And also that God hath set his hand and seal to change the times and seasons, and to blind their minds, that they may not understand his marvelous workings; that he may prove them also and take them in their own craftiness; Also because their hearts are corrupted, and the things which they are willing to bring upon others, and love to have others suffer, may come upon themselves to the very uttermost; That they may be disappointed also, and their hopes may be cut off; And not many years hence, that they and their posterity shall be swept from under heaven, saith God, that not one of them is left to stand by the wall. Doctrine and Covenants 121:5-15

3. New York City, Albany (New York), and Boston would be destroyed if they did not accept Mormonism (prophecy given in 1832) - Doctrine and Covenants 84:114,115

Nevertheless, let the bishop go unto the city of New York, also to the city of Albany, and also to the city of Boston, and warn the people of those cities with the sound of the gospel, with a loud voice, of the desolation and utter abolishment which await them if they do reject these things. For if they do reject these things the hour of their judgment is nigh, and their house shall be left unto them desolate. Doctrine and Covenants 84:114,115

A casual reading of the introductions of sections 105, 121, and 84 will reveal the historical particulars of these failed prophecies.

II Peter 2:1-3 is God's indictment of such a *prophet* as Joseph Smith

But there were false prophets also among the people, even as there shall be false teachers among you, who privily shall bring in damnable heresies, even denying the Lord that bought them, and bring upon themselves swift destruction. And many shall follow their pernicious ways; by reason of whom the way of truth shall be evil spoken of. And through covetousness shall they with feigned words make merchandise of you: whose judgment now of a long time lingereth not, and their damnation slumbereth not.

III.   THE FALSE RESTORATION

Joseph Smith taught that the true church had totally apostatized by his time, and that Gospel truth had been lost until he himself restored it through his revelations, teachings, and church.

Joseph Smith's greatness lies in the work that he did, the spiritual capacity he developed, and the witness he bore of the Redeemer. Since the keys of salvation were restored to the Prophet, it is in and through and because of his latter-day mission that the full redemptive power of the Lord has again become available to men. It is because the Lord called Joseph Smith that salvation is again available to mortal men. 'Joseph Smith, the Prophet and Seer of the Lord, has done more, save Jesus only, for the salvation of men in this world, than any other man that ever lived in it.' (Doctrine and Covenants 135:3). Mormon Doctrine, by Bruce R. McConkie, pg. 396

The scriptures teach plainly that the church never *totally apostatized* off the earth!

Jesus said

......I will build my church; and the gates of hell shall not prevail against it. Matthew 16:18b

Beloved, when I gave all diligence to write unto you of the common salvation, it was needful for me to write unto you, and exhort you that ye should earnestly contend for the faith which was ONCE DELIVERED unto the saints. Jude 3

Notice that the faith we are to contend for was *ONCE DELIVERED*, it was not *delivered then lost* to be *redelivered* later by Joseph Smith, or anyone else for that matter.

CONCLUSION

Joseph Smith restored nothing, he simply started a false religion based on HIM AND HIS MESSAGE. Since that message contradicts the message of the Bible, it makes Joseph Smith a false prophet and blasphemous boaster.

The lofty looks of man shall be humbled, and the haughtiness of men shall be bowed down, and the Lord alone shall be exalted in that day. For the day of the Lord of hosts shall be upon every one that is proud and lofty, and upon every one that is lifted up; and he shall be brought low: And upon all the cedars of Lebanon, that are high and lifted up, and upon all the oaks of Bashan, And upon all the high mountains, and upon all the hills that are lifted up, And upon every high tower, and upon every fenced wall, And upon all the ships of Tarshish, and upon all pleasant pictures. And the loftiness of man shall be bowed down, and the haughtiness of men shall be made low: and the Lord alone shall be exalted in that day. Isaiah 2:11-17

JESUS IS THE ONLY WAY

And as Moses lifted up the serpent in the wilderness, even so must the Son of man be lifted up: That whosoever believeth in him should not perish, but have eternal life. For God so loved the world, that he gave his only begotten Son, that whosoever believeth in him should not perish, but have everlasting life. For God sent not his Son into the world to condemn the world; but that the world through him might be saved. He that believeth on him is not condemned: but he that believeth not is condemned already, because he hath not believed in the name of the only begotten Son of God. And this is the condemnation, that light is come into the world, and men loved darkness rather than light, because their deeds were evil. For every one that doeth evil hateth the light, neither cometh to the light, lest his deed should be reproved. But he that doeth truth cometh to the light, that his deeds may be made manifest, that they are wrought in God. John 3:14-21

Jesus saith unto him, I am the way, the truth, and the life: no man cometh unto the Father, but by me. John 14:6

Chapter Eight
AN INVALID PRIESTHOOD

The Mormon church lays a great deal of emphasis on their supposed exclusive and divine authority, derived by an assumed acquisition of both the Aaronic and Melchizedek Priesthoods.

Article five of the Articles of Faith, by James Talamage, gives us an insight into THE IMPORTANCE THE MORMON CHURCH PLACES UPON THIS SUBJECT

Article 5 *We believe that a man must be called of God, by prophecy, and by the laying on of hands, by those who are in authority to preach the Gospel and administer in the ordinances thereof.*

Bruce R. McConkie sites the teachings of Joseph Smith, as well as Doctrine and Covenants to make his case.

This Melchizedek Priesthood comprehends the Aaronic or Levitical Priesthood, and is the grand head, and holds the highest authority which pertains to the priesthood, and the keys of the kingdom of God in all ages of the world to the latest

posterity on the earth; and is the channel through which all knowledge, doctrine, the plan of salvation and every important matter is revealed from heaven.

All other authorities or offices in the church are appendages to this priesthood...The Melchizedek Priesthood holds the right of presidency, and has power and authority over all the offices in the church in all ages of the world, to administer in spiritual things....The power and authority of the higher, or Melchizedek Priesthood, is to hold the keys of all the spiritual blessings of the church - To have the privilege of receiving the mysteries of the kingdom of heaven, to have the heavens opened unto them, to commune with the general assembly and church of the First-born, and to enjoy the communion and presence of God the Father, and Jesus the mediator of the new covenant. (D. & C. 107:5, 8, 18-19.) Mormon Doctrine, by Bruce R. McConkie, Pg. 476

Note the absolute and emphatic nature of McConkie's words in the following.

Without the Melchizedek Priesthood salvation in the kingdom of God would not be available for men on earth, for the ordinances of salvation-the laying on of hands for the gift of the Holy Ghost, for instance-could not be authoritatively performed. Thus, as far as all religious organizations now existing are concerned, the presence or the absence of this priesthood establishes the divinity or falsity of a professing church. It continueth in the church of God in all generations, and it administereth the gospel and holdeth the key of the mysteries of the kingdom, even the key of the knowledge of God (D. & C. 84:17-19), whom to know is eternal life (John 17:3.) If there is no Melchizedek Priesthood on earth, the true Church is not here and the gospel of Christ is not available to men. But where the Melchizedek Priesthood is, there is the kingdom, the Church, and the fulness of the gospel. Mormon Doctrine, by Bruce R. McConkie, Pg. 479,480

I. THE AARONIC PRIESTHOOD

The Aaronic priests were a holy and chosen group of priests (Numbers 16:5) ordained to exercise duties related to God's covenant.

Now therefore, if ye will obey my voice indeed, and keep my covenant, then ye shall be a peculiar treasure unto me above all people: for all the earth is mine: And ye shall be unto me a kingdom of priests, and an holy nation. These are the words

which thou shalt speak unto the children of Israel.
Exodus 19:5,6

Mormons cannot have the authority of the Aaronic Priesthood, for all their men are of the wrong tribe. God made it clear to Moses that only Aaron's descendants could hold the Aaronic Priesthood. Aaron was of the tribe of Levi. Mormons claim to be from the tribe of Ephraim or Manasseh. Therefore, they could NEVER rightfully hold the Aaronic Priesthood.

And thou shalt appoint Aaron and his sons, and they shall wait on their priest's office: and the stranger that cometh nigh shall be put to death.
Numbers 3:10

Furthermore Mormon priests have never fulfilled the biblical duties of the priest or the high priest in offering sacrifices (Exodus 29:38-44; Hebrews 5:1: 8:3). The priesthood cannot be separated from the sacrifices. But even if Mormon *priests* offered such sacrifices today, they would be of no value because the Levitical or Aaronic Priest was replaced and superseded by Jesus Christ, the Great Eternal High Priest (Hebrews 7:11-17; 10:8-21). He is now the only Mediator and High priest between God and man:

For there is one God, and one mediator between God and men, the man Christ Jesus. I Timothy 2:5

But this man, because he continueth ever, hath an unchangeable priesthood. Wherefore he is able also to save them to the uttermost that come unto God by him, seeing he ever liveth to make intercession for them. Hebrews 7:24, 25

Jesus saith unto him, I am the way, the truth, and the life: no man cometh unto the Father, but by me. John 14:6

The Mormon church teaches that nobody has the authority to baptize or preach the gospel unless he is ordained by someone who held the Aaronic Priesthood. Since the Aaronic Priesthood dissolved after the death, burial and resurrection of Christ, by their own admission then, the Mormons have no authority to preach or baptize!

II. THE MELCHIZEDEK PRIESTHOOD

Melchizedek is mentioned in Genesis 14:18-20 as a royal priest reigning in Salem. Our Savior is prophetically (Psalms 110) a Priest forever after the order of Melchizedek. According to scripture only Melchizedek held this priesthood in his day, and only the Lord Jesus Christ has ever had, or ever will have the priesthood after THE ORDER of Melchizedek.

The only way the Melchizedek Priesthood could pass from Christ to anyone else is for Christ to die, and REMAIN dead.

By so much was Jesus made a surety of a better testament. And they truly were many priests, because they were not suffered to continue by reason of death: But this man, because he continueth ever, hath an unchangeable priesthood. Wherefore he is able also to save them to the uttermost that come unto God by him, seeing he ever liveth to make intercession for them. Hebrews 7:22-25

The Mormon church commits BLASPHEMY when they claim to have a lock on the Melchizedek Priesthood. Only our Lord himself can claim the authority of the Melchizedek Priesthood. Christ is the High Priest over all New Testament born-again Christians, who are themselves part of a SPIRITUAL PRIESTHOOD described as *a royal priesthood*.

But ye are a chosen generation, a royal priesthood, an holy nation, a peculiar people; that ye should shew forth the praises of him who hath called you out of darkness into his marvelous light. I Peter 2:9

MULTIPLE HIGH PRIESTS?

Surely if Jesus Christ lives forever and is our High Priest, there is no need for other high priests. Thus, Mormon claims contradict the Bible at several points: there were *high priests* under the Old Testament Law, but nowhere does the Bible say they held the Melchizedek Priesthood; there were not multiple high priests, but only one legal high priest at a time, and priests had to be descendants of Aaron.

Today Jesus Christ is the only legal High Priest, but certain Mormon men claim they are high priests too. Hebrews 7:27-28 speaks of *high priests* because when one died he was replaced (Numbers 20:28; Hebrews 7:23). The Mormon Church has thousands of *high priests* today who are not descendants of Aaron, nor do they have the right to the Melchizedek Priesthood, so they cannot claim to have the same office of high priest. All of the *high priests* mentioned in the New Testament were a part of Judaism, not the church.

Mormon theology teaches that Joseph Smith had to have the priesthood before he could establish the church. But nothing in the Bible says that apostles, bishops, deacons, or any other New Testament office held either the Aaronic or Melchizedek Priesthood. So why did Joseph Smith need it? Nor does the Bible teach that the church or priesthood would need to be *restored*.

Once again, Mormon theology finds itself at odds with the Bible by insisting upon a *restored* New Testament priesthood that mirrors the obsolete Aaronic Priesthood, or presumes to usurp the exclusive authority of Christ's Melchizedek Priesthood.

In June, 1829, by divine appointment, Peter, James, and John came to Joseph Smith and Oliver Cowdery and conferred upon them the Melchizedek Priesthood. (D. & C. 27:12-13.) By the hands of Elijah and others of the prophets, also, an additional revelation of the priesthood was given, meaning that these ancient prophets came with keys and powers which authorized the use of the priesthood for additional purposes. (D. & C., 110:11-16; 128:17-21; Jos. Smith 2:38.) This priesthood - with all its powers, parts, keys, orders, and ramifications - is now fully operative among men. Again there is a kingdom of priests on earth, and the divine promise is that this situation will continue, the priesthood never again being lost. (D. & C. 65.) Mormon Doctrine, by Bruce R. McConkie, pg. 478

III. A MUDDLED ORIGIN

The Mormon church teaches that John the Baptist appeared to Joseph Smith and Oliver Cowdery and conferred the Aaronic Priesthood on them. The event is found in the Pearl of Great Price, Joseph Smith 2:68-73:

We still continued the work of translation, when, in the ensuing month (May, 1829), we on a certain day went into the woods to pray and inquire of the Lord respecting baptism for the remission of sins, that we found mentioned in the translation of the plates. While we were thus employed, praying and calling upon the Lord, a messenger from heaven descended in a cloud of light, and having laid his hands upon us, he ordained us saying: Upon you my fellow servants, in the name of Messiah, I confer the Priesthood of Aaron, which holds the keys of the ministering of angels, and of the gospel of repentance, and of baptism by immersion for the remission of sins; and this shall never be taken again from the earth until the sons of Levi do offer again an offering unto the Lord in righteousness. He said this Aaronic Priesthood had not the power of laying on hands for the gift of the Holy Ghost, but that this should be conferred on us hereafter; and he commanded us to go and be baptized, and gave us directions that I should baptize Oliver Cowdery, and that afterwards he should baptize me. Accordingly we went and were baptized. I baptized him first, and afterwards he baptized me - after which I laid my hands upon his head and ordained him to the Aaronic Priesthood, and afterwards he laid his hands on me and ordained me to the same Priesthood - for so we were commanded. The messager who visited us on this occasion and conferred this Priesthood upon us, said that his name was John, the same that is called John the Baptist in the New Testament, and that he acted under the direction of Peter, James and John, who held the keys of the Priesthood of Melchizedek, which Priesthood, he said, would in due time be conferred on us, and that I should be called the first Elder of the Church, and he (Oliver Cowdery) the second. It was on the fifteenth day of May, 1829, that we were ordained under the hand of this messenger, and baptized. Immediately on our coming up out of the water after we had been baptized, we experienced great and glorious blessings from our Heavenly Father. No sooner had I baptized Oliver Cowdery, than the Holy Ghost fell upon him, and he stood up and prophesied many things which should shortly come to pass. And again, so soon as I had been baptized by him, I also had the spirit of prophecy, when, standing up, I prophesied concerning the rise of this Church, and many other things connected with the Church, and this generation of the children of men. We were filled with the Holy Ghost, and rejoiced in the God of our salvation.

Several things in this account are quite confusing, John the Baptist is supposed to have conferred the Aaronic Priesthood on Joseph Smith and Oliver Cowdery who had not yet been baptized. Since Mormons believe baptism is necessary for salvation, they must have been unsaved sinners when they received the priesthood! Mormonism teaches that baptism must precede the receipt of the priesthood, so why didn't John the Baptist baptize them first? He had the authority since he had baptized the Lord (Matthew 3:13-16). Surely if the Spirit of the Lord could baptize Adam (Pearl of Great Price, Moses 6:64-65), the spirit of John the Baptist could baptize Joseph Smith. Instead,

John told Joseph Smith to baptize Oliver Cowdery, and Oliver Cowdery to baptize Joseph Smith. However, since Joseph Smith was unbaptized when he baptized Oliver Cowdery, Oliver's baptism was invalid by Mormon standards. Then Oliver Cowdery improperly baptized Joseph Smith, because since Oliver Cowdery's baptism was invalid, Joseph Smith's would be invalid also by Mormon standards. Next, Joseph Smith who was improperly baptized, conferred the Aaronic Priesthood on an improperly baptized Oliver Cowdery - a thing the Mormon church would reject today! Oliver Cowdery, who was improperly baptized and ordained, then conferred the Aaronic Priesthood on an improperly baptized Joseph Smith. But John the Baptist had conferred the Priesthood of Aaron on Joseph Smith and Oliver Cowdery before they baptized each other. Since they conferred the same priesthood on each other after they baptized each other, they must have lost it while baptizing each other. This also makes both baptisms invalid! Because Joseph Smith and Oliver Cowdery ordained each other after baptizing one another, they must have realized they didn't get any priesthood from John the Baptist, or if they did, they lost it. Either way they had no authority to baptize or ordain each other. Neither Joseph Smith nor Oliver Cowdery had the priesthood after they baptized each other. Otherwise it would have been foolish to ordain each other in order to give that which they already possessed.

Are we having fun yet? Are you thoroughly confused? The whole testimony of these two men sounds more like a circus side-show than a divine revelation.

IV. <u>TEMPLE WORK INVALIDATED</u>

An invalid Mormon priesthood disqualifies Mormon gospel preaching (by their own rules). Since their temple is consecrated through an invalid priesthood, all work done in Mormon temples is null and void. *Baptism for the Dead* (see chapter six) is also invalidated by Mormon rules. Temple marriages are not performed with the authority that many Mormons suppose. In fact, the whole superstructure of Mormonism collapses when its professed priesthood authority is exposed as a fraud. Why? Because Mormonism presupposes exclusive authority as a restored church, and validates its mission based on its priesthood.

It is easy to boast of great divine authority. But to

prove it is quite another thing. It is quite impossible to demonstrate that the Mormon priesthood was legitimately received, or that Mormons now possess it. The lack of biblical support, the confusion in their own record, and their inability to demonstrate this power or authority today is evidence that the Mormon church does not possess what it professes.

Whoso boasteth himself of a false gift is like clouds and wind without rain. Proverbs 25:14

In this book we have taken the up the challenge of Joseph Fielding Smith, Brigham Young, and Orson Pratt to examine the Mormon church. We have set about to inspect whether or not their teachings are consistent with those of the Bible. From its multiple authorities, to its polytheistic teaching of exaltation, its invalid priesthoods, all the way to its failed prophesies and bizarre view of Jesus and Lucifer – we can safely state that Mormon doctrine is not Bible doctrine.

My friend, salvation is found in Jesus Christ alone, and growth in Christ is found in the Bible.

Believe you are sinner in need of a savior (Rom. 3:23), that Jesus died and rose again to pay for the eternal penalty of your sins (Rom. 5:8, Rom. 6:23), and the best way you know, in prayer, accept Jesus Christ and the forgiveness that only He can offer (Rom. 10:9-13).   Do this, and you will be saved.